Victoria

Living with
BLUE & WHITE

Victoria

Living with
BLUE & WHITE

FROM THE EDITORS OF *VICTORIA*

83 press

Hoffman Media
2323 2nd Avenue North
Birmingham, AL 35203
hoffmanmedia.com

ISBN 9781940772905
Printed in China

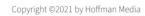

83 press

CONTENTS

Introduction

Rarely has the pairing of two hues captured hearts and imaginations like blue and white. Whether they are the basis for an interior design scheme, the focus of a gracious table, or the foundation of a serene vignette, these perennially adored partners sweep the spectrum, from tranquil shades as calming as a summer breeze to deep saturations as dramatic as they are inviting. Covering the full breadth of iterations, along with looks devoted exclusively to snowy alabaster, this breathtaking volume showcases myriad possibilities for enfolding the classic palette into one's home and lifestyle.

Since its inception, *Victoria* has lauded the charms of blue and white. We welcome readers into blissful retreats dressed in these sublime hues, from quaint cottages where cupboards overflow with petal-strewn textiles to grand manors arrayed with the finest antique furnishings. Our pages brim with collections of cherished heirlooms, including exquisitely embroidered linens, storied china patterns, and shapely porcelain finds. In a panoply of pretty spaces, we explore regional styles from French Country to coastal chic, savor the wonders of sea and sky in alfresco settings abounding with natural splendor, and offer guidance for cultivating both private havens for rejuvenation and rooms where families enjoy gathering. Finally, we demonstrate how accents of additional tints can blend harmoniously within the enduring appeal of a blue-and-white framework.

Reflecting on the magazine's longstanding devotion to this popular duo, our editors have curated the loveliest images from our extensive library of features, pairing rich photography with eloquent prose to bring you a treasury that bears distinct and undeniable hallmarks of the brand. Pure pleasure to peruse, the book is a celebration of timeless design intended to delight generations of readers. Whether one is just awakening to the aesthetic versatility of this color collaboration or falling in love with it all over again, *Living with Blue & White* is certain to enchant as well as inspire.

Welcoming
INTERIORS

Classic Comforts

No matter where we are in life, we tend to circle back to all our favorite things. Such is the case for one couple, even when it comes to houses. Having built three new homes during various stages of their lives, the pair always return to the aesthetics they hold dear, as well as to the local design professionals who have become like family. The openness and elegance of French Colonial style have remained constant inspirations, notes L. Craig Roberts, the architect who has worked with the couple for decades. "They wanted something very similar to the first house I designed for them in 1979," he says. "We even used a lot of the same drawings."

This most recent residence holds court just off the east shore of a small inlet in the Gulf of Mexico. Contrary to its overall newness, the structure captures a bygone era with earnest historical exactness. Spacious and breezy, a wide central hallway—once known as a dogtrot—runs the entire length of the house and opens onto every room of the main floor. Horizontal beadboard walls and soaring 12-foot ceilings expand the space visually, further strengthening its period grandeur. True to French Colonial design, all the living spaces run along one side of the home, with private rooms located on the opposite side. Quaint covered porches on the front and back of the house provide welcoming open-air verandas that nod to the neighborly gentility of a simpler time. Designed specifically to keep air circulating throughout, the house also features functional transoms above the doorways.

The home's classic color scheme was born from the owners' extensive assemblage of blue-and-white Chinese export porcelain. This enduring thread sews varying shades, from indigo and cerulean to the palest powder blue, into every corner of the environs. The presence of other distinguished finds adds to the dwelling's storied appeal, including intricate antique rugs, a breathtaking wall tapestry from Paris, and scores of symmetrically positioned accessories. Each item brings Old-World character, depth, and patina to one pristine room after another.

Interior designer David Erhardt, who worked closely with Craig on this project, as well as on the homeowners' prior residences, was also impressed with his clients' distinctive eye for design. Using a rich color palette based on the couple's collections of Imari and blue-and-white Chinese export porcelain, David created a series of opulent yet inviting spaces that connect effortlessly. Finishing touches—the kitchen's repurposed two-hundred-year-old brick floors recovered from a demolished site in Mobile, Alabama, and rough-hewn ceiling beams salvaged from Mississippi—lend texture and sincerity to the home's stately architecture.

"I wanted to be sure it looked collected and not decorated," explained David, who scoured Europe with his clients for exquisite home furnishings. Noteworthy finds include an antique Italian screen with meticulously hand-painted illustrations, a rare water-gilded Italian mirror, a hanging wall tapestry purchased in Paris, and a jewel-tone Lavar Kerman camel-hair rug that anchors the living room. A luscious layering of silk-brocade draperies and upholstery fabrics, plush custom-woven rugs, fine artwork, and a well-culled collection of decorative accessories impart a familiar warmth and coziness. The designer's signature accents include sturdy iron brackets that support the living room ceiling beams and vegetable-dyed raked-plaster wall panels in the kitchen, sitting room, stairwell, and upstairs study.

The home reflects the couple—"gracious and comfortable, eclectic and relaxed"—said David, who was diligent in maintaining Craig's architectural vision with the interior details. "They really let you do things right, and there's no greater honor than when clients trust you repeatedly," Craig says of the homeowners. "They really do become like family."

Located in a leisurely waterfront neighborhood, this grand home boasts more than just elegance—an attitude of tranquility mirroring the leisurely lifestyle of the coast also resides here. The living room's restful color palette is grounded by an elaborate antique Lavar Kerman rug made of camel hair. Similarly detailed patterns in the posh brocade armchair upholstery and mantel-mounted porcelain invite a sense of luxury to the space, while an overstuffed tufted ottoman posing as a coffee table eases the air of high formality. Comfort is king in these environs, where sumptuous textures grace the conversational seating, silk-canvas draperies cloak the edges of oversized windows brimming with natural light, and a fireplace beckons one to enjoy the warmth of a cup of tea and the comfort of family.

The interiors of this abode exhibit an innate sense of identity, unified by a lavishly relaxed style that feels perfectly at home within the sprawling architecture reminiscent of a French Colonial farmhouse. Refined collectibles are carefully placed and never cluttered, resulting in a poised and functional space that honors the past with elegance. Opposite: An oil painting titled *The Battle of Mobile Bay* hangs above a treasured set of silver. This page, below right and above left: Carefully engraved and embroidered, family monograms grace the face of serving pieces and textiles.

A custom-made barley-twist bed takes on regal stature dressed in a coverlet from Nancy Corzine and yards of pale blue brocade fabric from Cowtan & Tout. A taupe sofa shimmers with Bergamo Fabrics silk upholstery, and the faint blue walls have been treated with a hand-dragging technique to replicate the crisp look of linen. The pastel shade chosen for this refuge mirrors a clear, calm sky.

"Every blue plays well with every other blue, and the right shade can transport you from the rain-soaked English countryside to the Aegean Sea. It's a miracle color."

—Jonathan Adler

Cocooned in comfort, this master bedroom is cloaked in luminous silks, sumptuous brocades, and a custom Chinese Oushak rug. Placed before the four-poster bed and marked with a bouquet of tulips, a serene and sumptuous seating area offers space for winding down with a book before nightfall.

Beautiful Spaces

A forever favorite, blue-and-white captures the essence of blissful living in a perfect pairing of color. Whether used to furnish a room with treasured antiques or a bountiful bevy of tranquil blossoms, the shades used in these environs kindle joy wherever they are found. Opposite and above: In the sitting room, one homeowner creates a relaxing balance with warm wood furnishings by displaying her assortment of Chinese export porcelain. She advises other collectors to carefully shop for and choose the best pieces they can afford, asserting that it is better to have one fine piece than many things with no substance or quality.

Like the changing of tides, colors seem to take their turn in the public eye, swelling with popularity, saturating the markets of fashion and interior design, and eventually fading from prominence. But, as enduring as the sea itself, blue remains a tried-and-true favorite—especially when paired with gleaming alabaster. Opposite: Floral wallpaper and marbleized jars brighten a room where the icons of summer, hydrangeas, adorn canvases that hang above the very blooms that inspired them. Masterfully woven tablecloths add graceful softness to the setting, and design books inspire further use of the cherished combination of shades. *Blue & White and Other Stories: A Personal Journey Through Colour* by William Yeoward reveals the style maker's passion for color, while designer Beth Webb's *An Eye for Beauty: Rooms That Speak to the Senses* explores her approach to living graciously. In *Authentic Design*, architect and designer Lauren Rottet balances contemporary sensibilities with the traditional styles of history. This page, clockwise from above right: Hand-painted pillows create a comfortable nook for penning greetings to loved ones on patterned indigo stationery. The natural complement to a loose gathering of flowers in shades of blue and white, handfuls of greenery peppered with dashes of sparkling yellow bring summer's brightness to a charmingly uncomplicated arrangement.

In a guest room awash with hospitality, an understated wall color illuminates a four-poster bed dressed for company in sumptuous white linens. Treasured family portraits and porcelain keepsakes bring a warm sense of nostalgia to this inviting suite, while bouquets of vivid blue blooms extend a genial greeting to overnight visitors.

This page: Schumacher's classic Hydrangea Drape wallpaper in the Delft hue mixes beautifully with contemporary print pillows and lampshades in the guest room of one historic home. Opposite: Family photos and a darling pet make this house feel like home, but its thoughtfully placed blue-and-white accents bring about the thoughts of tranquility that help one find rest in a cheerfully well-lit atmosphere. Neutral shades of cream and beige complement the wooden furniture and its carefully carved details.

Opposite: Designer, author, and entrepreneur Carolyn Westbrook's dining room features pretty toile fabric in both curtains and framed panels. The pattern is similar to those on the table setting's transferware dishes—prized pieces that continue to catch Carolyn's eye. This page: This master bath exemplifies the philosophy held by the homeowners, that interiors "should feel collected over time and not staged." Among the treasures is an eighteenth-century carved-wood putto used as a towel valet.

Elegant Accents

Reminiscent of feathery clouds drifting
across an azure heaven, the classic palette of blue and white is timeless. No shortage of treasures bear these hues, for they are perfectly placed in any surroundings, from upon the table to beside the bed and beyond. Opposite: A delightful bouquet of peonies, tulips, and hydrangeas in these beloved shades is enhanced by the delicate damask of St. Antoine wallpaper from Farrow & Ball. Surrounding the display are colorful trinkets of the finest caliber. This page: Romantic floral fabrics, delicate lace trim, and a silky ribbon give signature flair to a bolster pillow.

Refreshing shades of this cherished colorway bring to mind our favorite summer landscapes of sea and sky. Like panoramas of the most beautiful coastal landscape, creamy hues blend with brilliant ocean waves, dressing every inch of blissful interiors with decorative pieces certain to inspire and delight. Above left: As soft as an afternoon breeze, a panel of French blue linen drapery is gracefully embellished with a cream appliqué design for effortless Old-World appeal. Placing such a pretty pastel shade on either side of the window allows one to frame the scenery outside in a way that evokes sunny blue-sky days no matter the weather. Above right: If the urge to create beauty for the home strikes, give decorative accessories dainty hints of blue and white with striped ribbon trims. Opposite: Cool to the touch, crisp pillowcases will have you drifting off to sleep in no time. Enjoy French Country bliss with a mix of patterns and styles perfect to suit any taste—whether one prefers the charm of muted stripes, the simplicity of freshly laundered white linens, or the intricate vibrancies of a bolder floral pattern.

"We all have one idea of what the color blue is, but pressed to describe it specifically, there are so many ways: the ocean, lapis lazuli, the sky, someone's eyes. Our definitions are as different as we ourselves."

—Sarah Dessen

Opposite: Painterly wallpapers cultivate romantic ambiance in myriad botanical patterns. Each carefully designed inch plasters the room in floral pageantry, while the cool and calming undertones of not only blue and white, but hints of green as well, remind one of Mother Nature's gentle touch.

Opposite: Victorian and Edwardian continental pillow shams of handkerchief linen with Valenciennes lace surrounds rest on a cutwork-and-embroidery linen duvet. This iconic style of textile evokes memories of days gone by. This page: Tied together with a charming blue-edged ribbon, decorative cushions from around the world feature a range of distinctive patterns.

Cool, calm, and inspired, refreshing fabrics and finishes in crisp shades of blue and white create quite a splash in pared-down and easy summer interiors. While stripes are a classic choice, more organic patterns find complement in these reproduction transferware tiles, opposite, which create an air of Tuscan elegance. For foolproof fabric layering, combine large, graceful prints with smaller-scaled geometric ones.

Above left: The dreamy hues of a seat cushion evoke images of the garden's glory, providing a cheerful counterpoint to this antique chair's dark frame. Above right: Demonstrating our long affinity for blue and white, a tea-themed wallpaper and border recall the *Victoria* Magazine at Home collection with Imperial Home Décor Group. Opposite: In designer Tessa Foley's master bedroom, a Thibaut pattern forms the background for framed bird prints from her native Belgium.

Gracious TABLES

Lovely Settings

*I*t is difficult to conceive of a color scheme more versatile than beloved blue and white when setting a table. These two hues span a spectrum of possibilities, whether a hostess wishes to convey a cheerful exuberance, a calming sense of serenity, or the very height of sophistication. Somehow, no matter the occasion, from a relaxed evening meal with family to the most elegant of gatherings, this palette always pleases.

Picture a farmhouse in the French countryside—sunlight dancing upon a pine dining table draped in a traditional Provençal cloth, woven in cobalt and cream threads, and laden with generations-old Limoges china in a like colorway. Extravagant hydrangea blossoms, in shades ranging from pale ivory to periwinkle, spill from a milk glass vase, completing this idyllic scene. Perhaps one dreams of delicate blue-and-white textiles where bouquets of cornflowers dance across a cottony background, while another may prefer the polish of bold indigo contrasting shimmering pearl. That's the beauty of this classic collaboration—it offers saturations to suit every style, every whim, every imagination.

The pages that follow form a pathway of inspiration for creating a gallimaufry of table settings, both formal and casual. From the classic appeal of fine china to the more modern approach of vibrantly hued dinnerware, there is a pattern to suit every generation and taste. All of the images that follow illustrate the immeasurable value of attention to detail—sometimes, a simple monogram or an exquisitely painted motif in the perfect shade of blue makes all the difference in the world.

A posy of fresh-cut flowers echoes the vivid character of a centerpiece of lush blooms. Carefully wrought stitches adorn the crisp white tablecloth and a coordinating napkin, offering snowy white fields for showcasing a bevy of blossoms on treasured china.

Relax with a soothing cup of tea amid a sea of calming tones. Above right: Herend's Chinese Bouquet teacups and saucers are ready for service atop an heirloom filet lace tablecloth that was meticulously handmade by two nuns in an Italian convent. A vintage monogrammed Madeira handkerchief brings a personable touch to the table. In varied groupings, Mottahedeh's Blue Lace demonstrates the ease of mixing patterns from different makers, eras, and styles. Below left: A pitcher, teacups, and saucers coordinate seamlessly with a transferware platter. Above left and opposite: Chargers provide a bold backdrop for the designs on Royal Crown Derby's Blue Aves pieces. The meandering motif is echoed in a hand-embroidered tablecloth and napkins. Varga's Athens Champagne flutes gleam in Cobalt Blue, alongside Reed & Barton Francis I silver flatware.

Opposite: Serving pieces boasting lively geometric patterns mingle harmoniously with Quimper ware and other pretties in this rustic wooden hutch. The scalloped silhouettes of vintage linens add another layer of interest to the display. This page: Draped over a chair, a cache of freshly pressed textiles awaits the next oportunity for use.

"There are connoisseurs of blue just as there are connoisseurs of wine."

—Sidonie Gabrielle Colette

Enveloped in an air of history, our table is set with Royal Crown Derby china in storied patterns dating back to 1894. Wallace Silversmiths flatware rests alongside, proudly bearing the iconic Napoleonic bee, evocative of emblems that decorated the monarch's coronation robes. Lamps, ginger jars, and a cachepot add to the room's regal atmosphere, demonstrating the homeowner's affinity for lovely porcelain finds.

This assemblage demonstrates the effectiveness of showcasing varying depths of color. The eye dances across our tableau, noting contrasts between an ethereal cloth that seems to float over the expanse and the boldly hued serving dish that grounds the scene. The addition of transferware rendered in pale blue invites one to pause for a moment's repose, while the gentle presence of mostly white dinnerware with accents of beading offers a lingering breath of tranquility.

Whether hung on the wall or placed on the table, the relaxed versatility of blue and white ensures a harmonious blend of styles, from French and English to Asian and Moroccan. Combining old and new pieces, no matter their origin, creates a pleasing montage of shape, texture, and design.

Tucked amid beautifully wrapped packages, Royal Crown Derby's gilt-edged Blue Mikado and Grenville patterns strike a celebratory note perfect for marking milestones from birthdays and graduations to engagements and anniversaries.

Opposite: This casual entertaining area features a handy buffet for serving guests and a painted white wall shelf for housing china. Accompanied by linens, teacups, and pitchers, a lighthearted choreography of blue-and-white plates takes center stage in the vignette. This page, above left: Since its introduction in 1775, the Royal Copenhagen collection of Blue Fluted patterns has remained popular for generations.

Opposite: Stunning vases mimic the look of *terre mêlée* (mixed earth), a style of marbled ceramic that originated in the eighteenth-century in Apt, a town in southeastern France. This page: Delicate etchings and the faintest hint of color draw attention to the gleaming Fostoria Navarre Blue goblets.

Alongside an antique sugar bowl, a richly detailed Staffordshire creamer, with its shapely form and elegant handle, still holds the power to enchant many years after it was crafted in Stoke-on-Trent, England. Pottery from this area continues to captivate collectors—especially when pieces boast our favored palette.

Splendid serving pieces, a veritable feast for the eyes, brighten a selection of tabletops set for tea and dessert. Clockwise from above left: Glass hobnail and satin-glass cake pedestals host elegant confections, while a teapot playfully alludes to its purpose, and porcelain cups, pots, and plates blossom with fanciful petals that exist not in nature but only in the imagination. Opposite: Treat yourself to a taste of garden grandeur with pitchers that showcase its spectacular offerings. Also use teapots, teacups, creamers, and sugar bowls to transform your china into beguiling containers for fragrant posies.

In Tessa Foley's New England–inspired dining room, an antique table and chairs pair with custom-made wing chairs. Print linens echo the tones of collected pottery. The interior designer loves the "instant feeling of history" imparted by timeworn treasures.

Pristine Linens

A collection of textiles—those thoughtfully
acquired pieces that lend softness to environs, create a mood, or call to mind a special memory—suffuses interiors with heart and soul. Esteemed for both their beauty and function, linens impart a gracious sense of welcome to the table. The joy of collecting springs from acquiring magnificent but discarded treasures and restoring their purpose as beloved elements for use and display. Humble or history-steeped, these are the layers that complete a home.

Opposite: United by color palette, this tableau comprises textiles of different styles, but each tea towel is noteworthy in its own right for pretty trimmings and expert handwork. Grouped together, the white-on-white ensemble creates a sum greater than its parts. This page: Wrought in navy thread, an interlocking script monogram adds flair to an ecru hemstitched napkin and place mat.

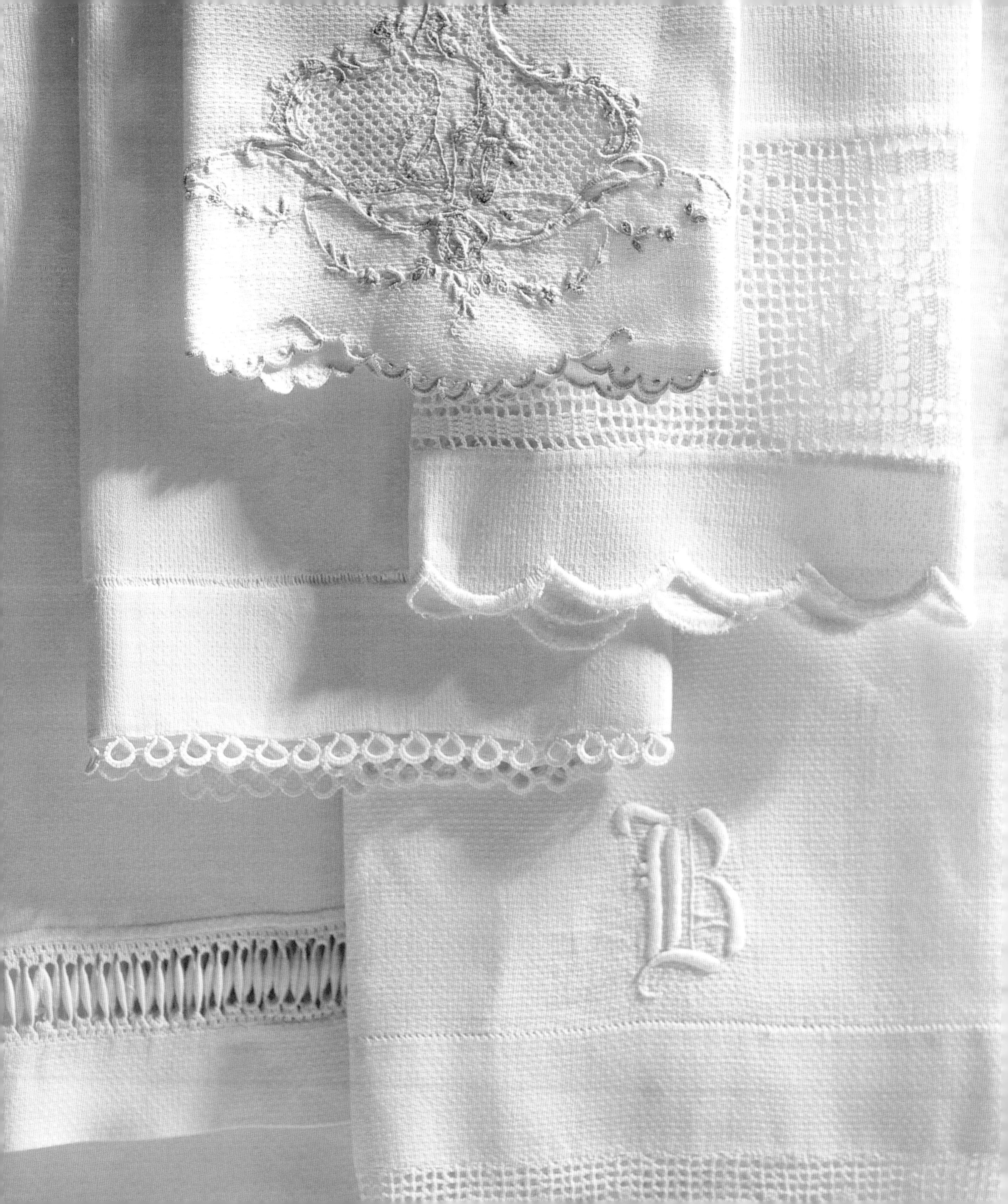

M. G. Spratt.
1894.

Enchantment can begin with a glance. One arresting example of stitchery can spark a fascination with needlework, while a single piece of extravagantly edged cloth can inspire an infatuation with linens. Opposite: This beguiling signature might pique curiosity for the provenance of a tablecloth, ultimately kindling a lifetime passion for collecting. This page, clockwise from above right: Although white embroidery on white linen is a historically favored selection, colorful textiles also bring delight. Antique damask napkins embellished with a lovely insignia in soft blue reflect the hue of vintage transferware.

Cottage CHARM

Blue & White Sanctuaries

The allure of dwelling in a quaint cottage, tucked amid hollyhocks and roses, prompts many a daydream of whiling away the afternoon puttering in the garden, baking tasty recipes in a snug kitchen, or settling before a stone hearth to read a classic tale. Escaping to such an abode may not be attainable for everyone, but whether one lives in a bungalow on the outskirts of town or a tiny *appartement* in Paris, it is possible to achieve the same cheery ambiance associated with cottage living by designing interiors around a blue-and-white palette.

Personal preference dictates whether one is drawn toward deep hues or softer shades, but pairing any blue with white is always a winning combination. Just consider the timeless appeal of ticking stripes and calico prints, Delft tiles and Wedgwood china, chinoiserie ginger jars and toile pastoral scenes—all favorite elements for this style of décor. The classic color couplet not only finds a place among a variety of regional looks, from French Country to coastal chic, it is also welcome in any room of the house. The palette is particularly well suited to a bedroom, where mixing patterns and textures can be interpreted in a sophisticated manner or in a delightfully homespun way.

While even a sprinkling of accessories in this much-loved theme brings beaucoup charm to a home, layers of linens, a collection of antique china, and the perfect floral wallpaper are bound to bring about pure blue-and-white bliss.

Snipping blossoms from one's garden is an easy way of introducing blue-and-white accents into the home. *Hydrangea macrophylla* varieties come in a range of hues, from snowy white to deep sapphire, with dozens of lovely shades in between, making them an ideal choice to incorporate into this pleasing color scheme.

There is undeniable strength of character in the well worn. Remnants from the past—cherished and storied—radiate incredible warmth and a sincere sense of purpose. Consider the allure of faded vintage fabrics, china pieces lovingly flawed from decades of use, and distressed surfaces paint chipped or rough hewn. To live among these age-old relics and heirlooms is to experience the heart of pure country style.

From the palest hints of periwinkle to the deepest saturations of indigo, blue in all its beautiful shades strikes a happy note in interior design schemes. When ninth-century artisans first brushed cobalt pigment onto pale earthenware, they launched a love for blue-and-white crockery that has abided for centuries. The lovely pieces in the cabinet, shown opposite, transcend mere utility to become eye-catching artistic displays. This page, above: Versatile striped ticking fashioned into accent pillows brightens a daybed and covers the seat of a lattice-back chair.

Above: Something as simple to assemble as a stack of chambray tea towels, a lavender nosegay, and a treasured antique plate becomes an enchanting vignette, especially when set against a bare-wood background. Opposite: Blue-and-white accents capture attention in this sweetly rustic bedroom, where a mélange of pretty cotton shams pairs with a muted gray-plaid coverlet, while a bouquet of hydrangea blooms and fern fronds nestles in an antique pitcher atop the wicker side table.

Azure skies with cotton-wisp clouds, freshly pressed pinstripe shirts, enchanting scenes depicted on Delft dinnerware—has there ever been a cheerier combination than blue and white? Easily incorporated into any genre of home décor, from French Country to Scandinavian to Early American, these complementary hues brighten interiors with their crisp contrast and classic style.

Opposite: With its washed-pine furniture and floral fabrics, a brimful office reflects Nantucket summer-cottage style. This page, below right: A pair of pillows abloom with roses and other posies beckons guests to a welcoming window seat. Above right: Stems of grape hyacinth slip into a weathered pitcher to form a lightly fragrant springtime bouquet.

A blue-and-white palette unifies a playful mix of patterns on these furnishings and accent pieces. Right: The buttery yellow background of a simple, gathered curtain complements the blue shades while offering its own cheerful note. Opposite: A quartet of topiaries flanks a generously sized ginger jar, creating a pleasing vignette atop a chest.

"Blue is the only color which maintains its own character in all its tones."

—Raoul Dufy

Ordinary watering cans in varying shades of blue double as impromptu vases for an exuberant array of fresh-cut flowers, gathered straight from the garden. A toile pillow bearing a rustic scene nestles among a medley of plump cushions in a selection of complementary patterns and fabrics.

Opposite: A few well-chosen accessories, like a fringed table runner and the blue-and-white china on the mantel, introduce subtle color in a quiet place. This page, clockwise from above right: Whether grand or elegantly spare, bedrooms should reflect the soul of their inhabitants. This light-filled retreat captures cool simplicity with nothing more than a pair of mismatched linen coverlets and two well-worn vintage pillowcases. Predominantly white décor may be given a visual boost with blue accents, whether it's a vase brimming with long-stemmed flowers, a simple wire basket cradling a pastiche of pretty tea towels, or a painted chest, scuffed from years of use and topped with a collection of woven-straw hats.

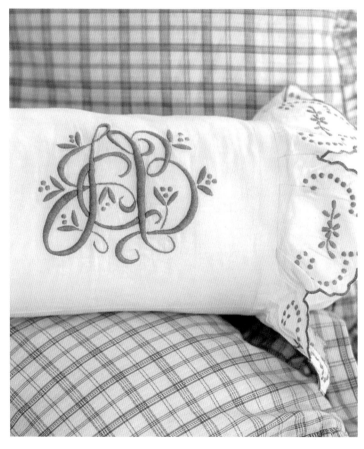

A merry medley of fabrics displays breezy appeal. Clockwise from below right: Cheerful plaid pairs with a pillow bearing initials sweetly entwined with blooms, while embroidered details trim crisp white curtains, and a laundry, brimming with winsome linens, makes everyday tasks infinitely more enjoyable.

A Light-Filled Retreat

This inviting home mixes traditionally refined architectural elements with sumptuous details in sun-drenched rooms made for casual, comfortable living. Balanced and unfussy, this interior design scheme by Phoebe Howard starts with a simple palette and finishes with a sense of beautiful livability. Using the same creamy wall color throughout makes the modest space feel more expansive.

Clean and straightforward, a white-on-white approach instantly brightens rooms and combines easily with shades of blue. Left: A splash of mellow blue-gray on the kitchen cabinets contributes a casually elegant touch, while the black wrought-iron light fixtures placed throughout the home create a unifying effect. Opposite: Family-friendly outdoor fabric gives sumptuous armchairs the bonus of handsome durability. The room's glass-front cupboard is both pretty and practical.

An Alabaster *Maison*

Whisper-soft pastels pair with myriad shades of white to impart pure tranquility to an apartment in Paris's elegant 9th arrondissement. This ethereal, sunlit sanctuary brims with romantic French treasures discovered in the City of Light's trove of antiques shops and *brocantes*.

An enchanting assemblage of long-cherished items, discovered on treasure-hunting excursions to the renowned Parisian markets, is not hidden away in cupboards but thoughtfully arranged in vignettes throughout the apartment. Stacks of old books mingle with religious figurines, while embroidered linens and vintage French teacups lend authentic charm to the tiny kitchen, where open shelving displays even more favorite finds. Mismatched chairs and a worn table hold generations of stories in the chipped paint and weathered wood.

A ceiling medallion mimics the reflection of light emanating from a crystal chandelier in the bedroom, a dreamy retreat swathed in creamy hues. Lace curtains filter sunlight pouring in from the floor-to-ceiling window and reflected by a pair of mirrors—one on the roomy, antique cupboard and another leaning against the wall. A mélange of vintage white linens dresses the bed, with a blue-floral pillow offering a nuance of subtle color.

The *Peaceful* PRESENCE of WHITE

In Hushed Tones

*A*s a layer of snow lends an ethereal feeling of serenity to the world outside, a palette comprising shades of white creates a vision of calmness within interior spaces. Much more than a one-note wonder, this color comes in an endless range of tints, with some leaning toward a whisper of yellow or pink and others bearing just the slightest hint of green, blue, or gray, ensuring an excellent choice for any need. In similar fashion to the feeling of awaking to discover a landscape transformed by fresh drifts, old spaces inspire wonder when refreshed with the gentle presence of alabaster.

A bright, sunny kitchen, complete with glossy white cabinetry and marble countertops, is a classic representation of the appeal of this ever-fashionable scheme, as is a bathroom where a pristine porcelain tub issues an enticing invitation to indulge in a soothing soak. Cloaked in creamy hues of ivory and vanilla in a range of textures, a master suite poses a welcoming sanctuary for sweet dreams, as well as the ideal place to start the day, well rested and composed.

Living spaces swathed in a symphony of snowy décor offer a relaxing refuge for quiet contemplation amid tranquil surrounds. Sink-down sofas, fluffed to perfection with downy pillows and knitted afghans in ecru and eggshell, speak to one's longing for a placid retreat, wrapped in hushed hues, where body and mind can be at peace.

There is no place that imparts such calm
sweetness as one adorned in the purity of white. Layers and ruffles of clean, crisp, sophisticated alabaster tell a story of simple beauty and grace. This narrative is especially welcome in private spaces, such as this boudoir, where a bouquet of roses lends natural fragrance to a dressing table laden with an array of scented offerings.

Homeowner and artist Judy Parsons adores color but is drawn to white. "It's so peaceful. Most people who are creative experiment with color," she says, "but they come back to a clean palette because it's so soothing." This page: Notice how Judy's collection of white and cream teapots, old and new, nestled in a Shaker-style hutch is vividly defined against walnut shelves.

"White ... is not a mere absence of color; it is a shining and affirmative thing."

—Gilbert K. Chesterton

The gentleness and simplicity of all-white bedding can be visually therapeutic, offering respite from the more colorful areas of a home's communal spaces. Behold our frilly and angelic interpretation, created with a romantic layering of pillows and linens from Pom Pom at Home. Founded by three Belgian natives, the linen company specializes in environmentally conscious products that embody casual elegance.

Our most captivating rooms often take on lives of their own amidst the trappings with which we furnish them. Created with light, shadow, and treasured objets d'art, these soulful compositions can capture our most intimate personal style. Varying textures and complementary colors in juxtaposition have the power to initiate divine visual balance. Such are the graceful curves of a tufted love seat and the slender cabriole legs of a nightstand situated against the sharp slant of a rustic beadboard ceiling or the classical refinement of a vanity table, chair, and mirror alongside surfaces of rough exposed brick.

Above: Framed by a romantic floral garland and other dramatic flourishes, an exquisitely rendered scene lends the look of toile to the painted bathroom vanity. Opposite: Wine and dine with lustrous Skyros Designs tabletop pieces, including deeply etched Lauren White Wine and Water Glasses in Clear and Historia Dinner Plates and Pasta/Soup Bowls in Paper White.

Interior designer Tessa Foley's goal for any client is to create a place that is warm and welcoming, one that allows the owners to retreat from the busy world, celebrate special times, and cultivate cherished memories. Opposite: She gave this kitchen a cottage-style makeover, complete with pleated stool covers and simple Roman shades. This page: Pretty textiles are oftentimes the first step for a new project, and these samples demonstrate the impact of including a variety of fabrics, textures, and embellishments.

To impart a sense of heritage to interiors, source monogrammed sheets from antiques shops and flea markets. "Why buy something new when there are so many wonderful things already out there?" one collector remarks. While some shoppers look exclusively for their own initials, many focus more on quality of craftsmanship or the beauty of a perfectly stitched cipher.

Inspirations of SEA & SKY

Seaside Style

A gentle shushing of waves, curling at the shore's sandy edge, draws attention to the play of frothy white foam upon the translucent turquoise water. Gazing out to the horizon, an almost imperceptible line divides the inky ocean from the azure sky above, where alabaster clouds drift leisurely along on the breeze. One of the reasons a sojourn to a coastal destination is always so alluring is the restful blue-and-white palette that flows throughout these halcyon surroundings.

Bringing the hues of the sea and the sky into one's own décor and tablescapes is a simple way to re-create moments of bliss, whether it is evoked through a heaping bowl of sea glass gathered while beachcombing or by a room painted the same celestial shade that added the grace note to a perfect summer day. The versatility of this color pairing is virtually endless, as it lends a serene or sophisticated note wherever it goes. Nautical blues run the gamut from icy aqua to true navy, while the heavens inspire not only the softest hints of mist but also the deepest jewel tones, like those found in sapphire and lapis.

Whether along the shore or just beyond our front doors, design inspiration abounds in nature and often is found in the very places that fill our hearts with joy.

The soft sound of the ocean as it gently laps against the sand gives a distinct and tranquil cadence to a sunset dinner. As mellowing light bathes the scene in radiance, settle in for a relaxing evening of mouthwatering fare surrounded by nature's warmest and most soothing embrace. Seashells and starfish sprinkled about the scene remind us that life abounds here.

A balm for the spirit, precious hours spent on the ocean or whiled away with toes in the sand take their place among the dearest of memories. Treasures imbued with the colors, sense of movement, and breezy style of that tranquil environment transport us back to the water's edge. Opposite: Stylized motifs take center stage on living room pillows, accented by feminine ruffles that mimic the texture of cresting waves. This page, clockwise from above left: A flattering silhouette and summer-perfect stripes strike just the right notes in this seaside ensemble. Moulded chocolates look even more enticing atop Vista Alegre Transatlântica china. Shapely vessels top a buffet, echoing the hues of the nautical print on a nearby chair.

Life on the coast offers unending views of windswept beaches, clear blue skies, and mesmerizing currents breaking along the shore. Hence, our seaside spaces tend to take cues from the environment when it comes to the colors we choose. Ethereal whites mix with the refined neutral shades of bamboo, and wicker pairs with soft blue linens to mimic the briny depths beyond—these timeless looks are forever soothing to the eye, calming to the soul, and encouraging to the heart.

A wicker love seat, positioned alongside furniture slipcovered in crisp alabaster twill, enhances the beachy look of whitewashed cabinets and beadboard paneling. This clean, colorless palette is the perfect foil for nautical accents, as well as blue-and-white fabrics in plaids, stripes, and solids. While shady palm trees wave in the breeze just outside, the smell of the ocean and the light reflecting off the sand make their way into restful environs like a sailboat coming into the harbor.

Oceanic landscapes reveal many natural tones that can be incorporated into romantic fabrics, unforgettable tabletop accessories, and storied collectibles. Mimic the hues of sand, sea, and sky with gauzy slipcovers, blue-and-white pillows, billowing azure linens, and opaque tableware reminiscent of sea glass. A mingling of shells, starfish, and handfuls of summery blooms adds even more of the earth's beauty to these vignettes. Whether displaying them beside an alfresco meal, at an outdoor reading nook, or within the home, these treasures complete a coastal scene.

"The sea! The sea!
The open sea! The blue, the
fresh, the ever free!"

—Bryan Procter

A seafairing theme navigates its way throughout the buoyant interiors of a breezy abode. Just a short walk from the beach, the coastal home offers waves of inspiration in the form of blue-and-white interiors. Ships sail across two decorative plates, while a shell-adorned box echoes the ocean's beauty.

Opposite: In this living room, an antique handmade pond boat, crafted in 1858, rests alongside a trio of vintage sailing trophies from the early 1900s. The seating area, defined by a seagrass rug placed atop quarter-sawn oak floors, features a sofa upholstered in classic linen. Bold patterns in the drapery, pillows, and porcelain lamps add an exciting vibrance to the tranquil room, calling to mind the sea's tendency to be turbulent at times and calming at others. This page, above left: The entryway's marble-topped bombe chest, painted with a pastoral Asian scene, serves as a base for a gilt mirror. Above right: While there is much to enjoy about the balmy ocean climate, true seafarers long to face the open waves around the world. Miniature globes and romantic paintings aid that dream while also accentuating the theme of nautical heritage that seems to swell throughout these light-filled environs.

Opposite: In a guest room, patriotic-themed needlepoint pictures top twin beds dressed in cheerful prints. The pale shade of blue paint anchors these varying hues and patterns found atop alabaster quilts. A pair of turtle shells hang from the wall, reminding visitors of the creatures that teem in and around the ocean. This page: Resting beside shelves of time-steeped books and collected coral, antique telescopes and binoculars aid in watching out for approaching weather—an important habit for any sailor.

In Nantucket and other coastal destinations throughout New England, seaside living does not equate to summery weather all year long. During colder months, this living room is warmed by a brick fireplace adorned with vintage artwork and blue-and-white pottery. The walls, floors, and seating create a sandy neutral palette upon which touches of pearly hued flowers, ocean-blue pillows, and brimming bowls of shell collections thrive.

Plein Air Pleasures

There is no substitute for the sense of refreshment one experiences while inhaling the bliss of nature. Especially when adorned with creature comforts and botanical trinkets, our most loved spaces offer respite for times spent entertaining or relaxing in the open air. Above: Set in a garden on Prince Edward Island, a handcrafted cerulean shed serves as this haven's backdrop.

In divine conspiracy with nature, hydrangeas proclaim the gleeful arrival of summer with their large bursts of silky petals and a painter's palette of extraordinary hues. Our favorite varieties, flowering forth in oversize clusters, are dressed in perfect shades of blue and white, calmly and proudly proclaiming a sense of elegance while still epitomizing the carefree temperament of the season. As balmy weather invites us to imitate nature's beauty in an outdoor work space, summer's spirit soars.

As seasonal sunshine causes the world around us to unfold its splendor, our hearts long to spend time in an outdoor oasis. On this shaded porch, the amenities of home are transported into such a paradise, warming the soul with perfectly stitched handmade quilts and colorful rugs. These vintage versions drape the furnishings with enchanting patterns of old, softening seating and encouraging guests to linger while enjoying the respite of a lazy afternoon.

Pairing two of nature's most prominent shades, summer paints everything in blue and white, surrounding us with the blissful hues of clear sky and softly billowing clouds, of pristine ocean and breaking waves, and of breathtakingly vibrant blossoms, such as these bountiful hydrangeas. As mysterious as they are beautiful, these leafy seasonal favorites have the ability to change color depending upon the environment in which they grow. The brilliant blue varieties often appear if there is aluminum present in the soil, while the contrasting snowball white version may thrive in a garden with varying acidity levels. Unlike the flamboyant mophead blooms, shown this page, lacecap hydrangeas, opposite, exude a wispy, feminine mystique with their spare and graceful composure. When arranging and caring for a hydrangea bouquet, place the fresh cuttings in cold water immediately, mist blossoms daily, and soak them for a few short minutes upon any wilting. This page, above: Tucked into the wide brim of a romantic hat and beneath the bow of its tenderly tied ribbon, one charming blossom offers fragrant charm to an ensemble worn at a summer picnic. The seating boasts remarkably accurate likenesses of the flower. Left: Never short of beauty, the hydrangea offers unmistakable appeal to whatever environs it graces.

Opposite: Floral motifs dance on a tablecloth in shades of indigo—atop which sit an assemblage of decorative vases in an eye-catching centerpiece. Brimming with blue-and-white flowers and bathed in the light of the sun, each porcelain treasure boasts exquisite detail, which abounds at this colorful fête. This page, above: Featuring a geometric border, an Hermès Bleus d'Ailleurs plate provides pleasing contrast to the natural motifs on Gien Oiseau Bleu china.

Opposite: June evenings were tailor-made for alfresco dining. Bermuda shutters filter late-afternoon rays while admitting blissful breezes to this graciously appointed porch. Dressed in summery blue-and-white hues, the rustic dining table beckons guests. This page: In the nearby garden, mophead hydrangeas offer the makings for a just-cut floral centerpiece. Planting these blossoms near the door invites summer inside.

What better way to serve a favorite brew beneath the blue heavens than in a teapot brushed with romance of the same shade? This antique pattern, Pivoines Bleues, was established in 1875 by Gien and features hand-painted peonies that echo the blossoming days of summer. Enjoy a cup in the company of a favorite book or friend.

Opposite: Our natural urge to bring the outdoors into the abode is reflected in the homelike atmosphere of our porches, pavilions, and verandas. Bedecked with lush boxwoods, potted ornamental trees, and other greenery, our open-air spaces connect us with nature and celebrate the allure of the garden. This page, above left and below right: A ruffled throw pillow softens the line between interiors and the outdoors, creating comfort in these temperate environs. Below left and above right: With a bountiful picnic, welcome those who would share this oasis by serving tea, fresh fruit, or sweet treats.

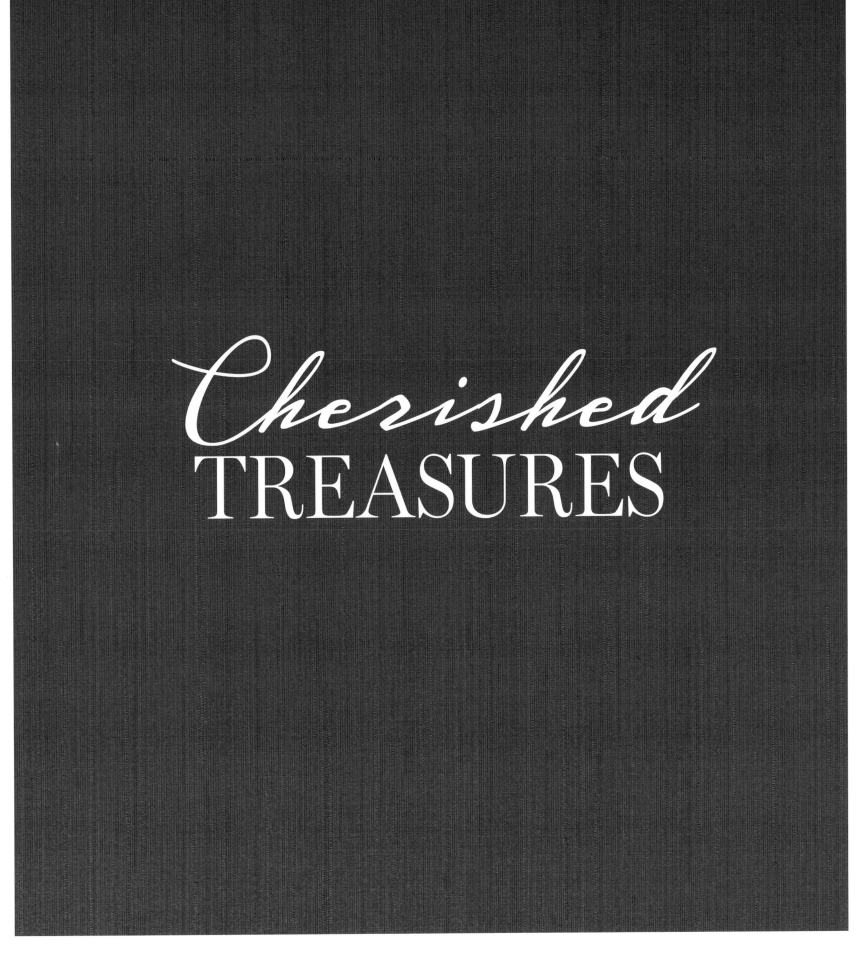

Cherished TREASURES

Gathering Heirlooms

W ho can explain exactly why certain objects tug at one's heartstrings? When considering the appeal of collecting dishes, it might be a favorite color or a pleasing shape that catches the eye—or maybe the allure is wrapped up with memories of Sunday dinner at Grandmother's house, when the table was set with her cherished Spode china.

Whether it is the brilliant cobalt-and-cream patterns found on transferware or the softer shades seen in Wedgwood's neoclassical-inspired Jasperware, the blue-and-white color combination is a favorite among collectors, who find it virtually impossible to limit their acquisitions to just a few pieces. The old adage, "the more the merrier," rings quite true here, for what could be prettier than an entire cabinet brimming with items in this prized palette?

Others find their passion lies with the elegant simplicity of milk glass, with its pure alabaster hue and frills of feminine details, or they are drawn to ironstone, the sturdy ceramic offerings that come in a range of colors, from bright white to cream, and evince a versatility that allows them to fit in with myriad styles, from country to modern. Regardless of one's preference, these lovely treasures bring delight to collectors and add immeasurable charm to their homes.

Distinctive blue-and-white transferware
known as *flow-blue* was once considered factory "seconds." During production, the color sometimes ran ever so slightly, softening the outlines and giving the motifs a hazy appearance. Blurring the lines between imperfection and brilliant design, within time, this type of pottery became a much-beloved addition to the table.

Left: Of the three flow-blue treasures displayed here, the most eye-catching is a Minton meat platter featuring the figure of a turkey. The uppermost piece is by Copeland & Garrett, while the design just below that hails from Rose and Garland. Motifs vary widely for flow-blue china, with some dramatic presentations. Opposite: A punch bowl by Spode illustrates an elaborate sporting scene—a sharp contrast to the simple banded cups and plates stacked beside it.

Flow-blue is found in a pleasing variety of patterns that fall into four categories: pastoral scenes, Oriental motifs, florals, and brushstroke, which employs a hand-painting technique rather than the usual transfer process. The William Brownfield pitcher, above left, dates to 1860, while a unique gadroon edge embellishes the circa 1849 plate, above right. A covered dish, center left, is an example of the floral category; the teapot to the right bears the Grecian Scroll pattern. A reticulated chestnut basket, below right, is a particularly pretty piece.

As elegant as a landscape resting silently beneath fresh frost and with patterns as unique as the individual flakes that fall gracefully from the heavens, the alabaster treasures known as milk glass have remained icons of style since their debut long ago in Europe. Pieces prior to the 1950s can be identified by the "ring of fire" test— when held up to natural light, vintage items will glow pink, green, or gold around the edges.

Originating in sixteenth-century Venice, milk glass gained popularity in Victorian-era France as an affordable alternative to porcelain before becoming a staple within wealthy American homes. Manufactured stateside by companies such as Westmoreland, Kemple, and Fenton, the majority of pieces on the market today were made during the material's revival after World War II. Items may be hand-blown or formed with a mould, and textures range from sharp and defined, such as the diamond sawtooth on a Westmoreland compote, shown above right, to subtle and classic, like the hobnail on Fenton bud vases, below left. Above left: Floral-rimmed dishes mingle among spoon rests, soup bowls, and lattice-edged plates.

One of the most cherished patterns among the plethora of blue-and-white dinnerware is Blue Calico by Burleigh, a company located in Stoke-on-Trent, Staffordshire, England—an area historically recognized as the heart of British ceramic manufacturing. The line's cheerful floral motif can be found on hundreds of different shapes since its inception in the 1960s, although the Chinese porcelain that inspired its look dates to two centuries earlier.

Blue Calico comprises a wide variety of items, from the usual components of traditional place settings to teapots, butter dishes, and more. Because each piece is made by hand and bears the distinctive touch of the individual decorator—along with the Burleigh backstamp—collectors know they are getting one-of-a-kind treasures. It is especially poignant to collect pieces that exemplify the skills of dedicated craftspeople—time-honored talents that connect them to generations of dedicated artisans.

A timeless go-to for the tabletop, whiteware has the power to freshen even the bleakest days of winter. Recreate this look with a creamy blend of classic contemporary pieces, antique porcelain, vintage ironstone, and bespoke monogrammed linens. Mixing past and present becomes effortless, as new pieces that capture traditional style provide a tasteful complement to antique embroidered napery.

Sleek white ironstone enhances almost any décor—from cottage to country, traditional to modern. Graceful pitchers and thick platters mix beautifully with contemporary-style dishes. Opposite: Embossed patterns featuring grains, flowers, and leaves distinguish these pitchers made in the 1850s and 1860s. Introduced by Staffordshire potters as a durable, affordable substitute for porcelain, the unadorned stoneware garnered instant favor in America for everyday use, spurring a heyday of mass production from 1840 to 1870.

"Beauty of style and harmony and grace and good rhythm depend on simplicity."

—Plato

English white ironstone has enjoyed the admiration of Americans for its charmingly simple appeal since it was first imported in the nineteenth century. It has a goes-with-anything style that elicits as much enthusiasm among modern-day collectors as it did with their forebears centuries ago.

The ability to identify English ironstone comes with experience and knowledge, as well as a practiced eye. Some pieces bear a distinguishing mark, although others do not. Color also provides the clues about age and origin: Newer American-made examples appear creamy white when compared with earlier authentic English pieces that possess a snowy white or barely blue-gray hue. Sturdy and versatile dinnerware, tea services, chamber sets, and other utilitarian white ironstone fulfilled nineteenth-century Americans' dreams of pristine table settings and home embellishments. Today, particular patterns evoke the passions of many collectors seeking something specific to match great-grandmother's dishes, while others acquire less-than-perfect examples that simply call to their hearts.

The classic designs of Josiah Wedgwood have graced tabletops and adorned homes throughout the world for centuries, boasting a wealth of remarkable history and marvelous detail. Sought after for its inspired artistry and elegance, his iconic pattern, Jasperware, was quickly embraced by the public and became his greatest triumph. Crafted in a rich shade of blue and adorned with white neoclassical motifs, the pieces retain their timeless sense of charm and are still prized today.

Enchanting pastoral scenes play across the lovely plates and platters of the pottery pieces known as *transferware*. The name refers to the process of transferring the print from an inked copper plate to paper that is then applied to the item; the paper burns away when pieces are fired. Dating to the mid-eighteenth century, the earthenware traces its origins to the famed Staffordshire area of England, where ceramic greats, such as Josiah Spode and Josiah Wedgwood, turned out the colorful pieces to the delight of a worldwide audience.

Personal
HAVENS

Moments of Bliss

In a world that moves at a faster pace than ever before in history, it is essential to one's well-being to pause from all the hurriedness and make time for renewing the spirit. Stepping away from responsibilities may seem like an indulgence, but an investment in serenity pays great dividends in a healthier mind, body, and spirit. While being whisked away to a private retreat might not be in the realm of possibilities, creating a semblance of such certainly is.

Finding a place for quiet contemplation could be as simple as a bed fluffed to cozy perfection with a dozen pillows and an heirloom quilt, worn soft by years of cuddles, or a passed-down vanity brimming with lotions, potions, and family pictures in silver frames. Perhaps it is a room that catches the morning sunlight or a nook holding an antique desk where generations of ladies have penned their correspondence. Whatever space speaks to your soul, turn it into your inner sanctum by filling it with all the lovely things that fill your heart with bliss.

Drawing a bath always has been a tranquil means of escape. The addition of fragrant bath salts leaves water silken and soothing, turning an everyday ritual into a transcendent experience. Make moments spent there a special occasion by treating yourself to all the little luxuries that dwell in your dreams.

Render a still life of peaceful beauty by bringing fresh flowers to the bedroom. A deep layering of pillows provides gentle comfort in a sumptuous nest of color, pattern, and texture. Solid hues and blue stripes merge harmoniously with neutral linen Euro shams and a "petaled" white-rosette accent cushion. For quick warmth, drape blankets at the foot of the bed.

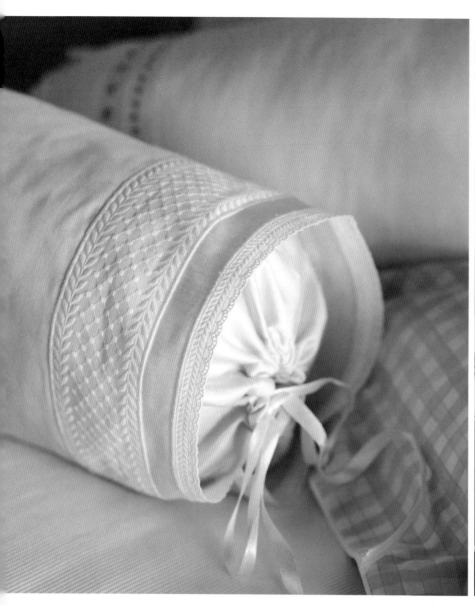

Quiet activities enjoyed in solitude, such as reading or writing, have a calming effect that often invites slumber. Pair these leisurely pursuits with a cup of hot tea for ultimate relaxation. An antique mahogany writing slope embellished with mother-of-pearl inlay, above right and opposite, features a leather top and several compartments to hold all the necessities. To create a cozy atmosphere of elegance and refinement, simple creature comforts should be kept bedside for ease of use. Essentials include a well-dressed bolster pillow and a leather-bound anthology of classic literature. Don't be afraid to blend bold patterns within a serene palette of blue and white.

Opposite: Meal planning is infinitely more enjoyable when undertaken in beautiful surrounds and accompanied by tea and pastries. A pretty volume keeps cherished family recipes close at hand. This page, above left: With a fire dancing ever so cheerfully at the hearth, snuggle down in a velvety cushioned chair near the warmth, pour a cup of Earl Grey, and mentally plan the upcoming spring garden. Below left: For a hint of all the botanical largesse to come, purchase dozens of flowers in your favorite hues from the local florist, and practice the art of flower arranging.

"Blue color is everlastingly appointed by the deity to be a source of delight."

—John Ruskin

A whimsical coronet only adds to the regal charms of a bed arrayed with a panoply of lovely pillows. Hues range from white to French blue, with paler shades, including a gentle taupe, lending softness to the assemblage. The color of the monograms echoes that of the stitching on a nearby bolster.

Left: An ornate Spode Blue Italian teacup and saucer rests atop a Madeira handkerchief. Opposite: Ever since the late seventeenth century, when simple boxes used for holding cosmetics and such were replaced with specialized furniture, the vanity table has been sacrosanct in a woman's life. Simply sitting here instills instant calm, as each passed-down heirloom is handled with reverence, and childhood memories of sampling the marvelous powders and perfumes in Mother's cache are recalled with such sweet fondness.

Sweet dreams come easily with a restful blue-and-white color scheme in the boudoir. Opposite: Ruched and ruffled white bed linens are the perfect foil for a lively floral duvet cover. A monogrammed pillow, along with sheets and pillowcases that are accented with delicate embroidery, invite luxurious sleep. A mini-print pillow provides an eye-pleasing balance of patterns. This page, above right: A seersucker robe promises ideal comfort for a summer day.

Opposite: Nestle into a field of wildflowers with D. Porthault bedding. Yves Delorme sheets add luxury, while prized books and a bouquet arranged atop a silver tray encourage relaxation. This page, clockwise from above left: Handcrafted jewelry spills from Chinese Bouquet pieces from Herend. Rendering a suite of monogrammed stationery in blue doubles its classic appeal, and keeping supplies close at hand in a pretty chest encourages one to pause to pen a few lines of correspondence. Wrapping stems with a pale purple ribbon complements the deeper tones of a handful of wildflowers. Wherever it is placed, the delicate posy is certain to add a welcome grace note.

This light-filled, dreamy bedroom tableau is based on a serene palette of blue and white. Elegant in its simplicity, the quiet vignette achieves artful impact with just a few complementary accessories. A well-furbished linen closet is a thing of beauty and often a treasure trove of meaningful heirloom collectibles, including lace-trimmed bedding, pillowcases, and quilts. Hand-stitched monograms personalize any space and can mix effortlessly with prints and patterns.

Bathed in Luxury

Whether cultivating a space for guests or
creating a haven for one's own daily use, consider thoughtful ways to ensure that moments spent here are truly worthwhile.
Along with the requisite cache of fluffy towels and pampering toiletries deemed necessary for such a retreat, the addition of
furnishings more often associated with other areas of the house—note the pretty French-style chair, sweetly proportioned
occasional table, and gilt-framed dressing screen shown opposite—may imbue these quarters with the ideal sense of luxury.

A place of sublime tranquility, the bathroom holds all the necessities for our beauty and bath rituals. Take time to compose artful vignettes of meaningful and useful accessories—vintage perfume bottles, posh towels, and antique vanity accoutrements—to create a sense of calm and continuity. Adding a sumptuous pair of slippers, below right, and a couple of wispy gowns, opposite, ensures that the space affords lingering comforts.

Illuminated by the warm glow of candlelight, or shadowed amid a sublime stream of natural light, antique treasures radiate an undeniable nostalgia when placed in artful compositions throughout our interiors. Within these restful private spaces, silver vanity heirloom accessories, monogrammed linens, delicate laces, and lustrous ceramic pieces capture the hushed beauty of a still life painting and provide our most intimate rooms with a distinguished signature mark.

Give your bathroom a seasonal makeover with accessories that mimic the soft hues of a summer sky. Above left: Whispers of blue from a Limoges box, as well as an embroidered fingertip towel and coordinating tissue holder, bring elements of softness to a vanity display. Above right: Spa accessories perfect for a getaway to distant shores include a flower-adorned hand towel, a monogrammed makeup bag, and skin-soothing moisturizers. Opposite: Corralled atop a pretty tray, decorative accents and a mix of fragrant soaps evoke a peaceful aura in the powder room.

Blue, White & FRIENDS

Cheery Complements

M uch like a strand of pearls sets off a little black dress, the introduction of an accent color to a blue-and-white design brings new dimension to this traditional scheme. While the beloved pairing would never be considered the shy and retiring type, the esteemed duo can play a role similar to a neutral background, allowing a tertiary hue to catch the eye's attention and elevate the whole setting.

Yellow is a particularly buoyant addition, as it offers a striking contrast to the main motif. Anyone who has placed a bowl brimming with lemons amid a setting of Blue Willow china can attest to that— it's like the sun shining in a bright summer sky. Pink has a comparable effect. A rosy hue is instantly uplifting and bestows a decidedly feminine touch, whether the selection is a bold splash of fuchsia or a whisper of blush.

Paler tints work their own sort of magic, melding beautifully with softer shades of cornflower and cream or offering a subtle backdrop for brighter hues. When paired with delicate greens, such as celadon or mint, lighter blues take on a soothing feel, ideally suited for lending tranquility to a setting. Whatever mood one wishes to create, a blue-and-white palette—with help from its colorful companions—strikes just the right note.

A white tablecloth, plates, and compote join blue linens and clear goblets to create a blank canvas for seasonal expression. Transforming the look is as easy as replacing the runner and centerpiece to reflect the latest gifts of nature's bounty.

Above: Summer days lend themselves to rejuvenating moments enjoying the comforts of bed late into the morning. This restful haven, dressed in supple linens and stylish accents, gets a boost of energy with the addition of cheery sunflowers. Opposite: Indigo damask linens adorn a table crowned with a pale-tone floral arrangement of lush roses. Heavy silver cutlery and gold-rimmed goblets frame plates of creamy white stoneware, creating a cultured air and a welcoming ambiance.

In interior designer Marsha Mason's master bedroom, Braemore Garden Toile fabric provides a sunny backdrop for a mix of D. Porthault, Ralph Lauren, and Charmajesty linens. Cherished antiques include a nineteenth-century oil pastel portrait, an exquisite trumeau, and silver dressing table pieces.

Opposite: Awash in tranquil hues of blue and ivory, cloud-soft bedding creates a soothing sanctuary. Sumptuous yellow accents illuminate the setting like rays of sunshine peeking through a stormy summer sky. This page, above: Natural inspirations brighten quiet corners. Here, tulips lend vibrant character to a fresh-cut bouquet.

Set against deeper shades, such as cobalt and royal blue, yellow becomes a vibrant partner, echoing the brilliance of the bold hue, and white allows both colors to shine. Handfuls of irises and daffodils lend springtime beauty to a collection of stemware and vases, right, while a gathering of blooms and citrus fruit brings convivial charm to a table set for serving lemonade, opposite.

Opposite: Johnna Bush's hand-painted mural, awash in tranquil shades of blue and green, forms the dining room's ethereal background. The table is set with Anna Weatherley china and features a silver epergne from President Howard Taft's White House. This page, above: The same color scheme evokes a restful feel in the bedroom of interior designer Tessa Foley.

Opposite: Throughout this residence—in every room, on every tabletop, and upon every shelf—pieces of meaningful provenance stand in distinction, poised to reveal their stories. The living room, a quiet oasis of blue-and-white toile with touches of green, gives sanctuary to several heirlooms passed down to the homeowner, including her grandmother's antique English walnut chest, her mother's prized burled-walnut secretary, and a virtual sea of earthenware and porcelain acquired over the years by the family of antiques enthusiasts.

Interior designer Carolyn Westbrook has built a brand—
and a home—around the subtle blending of vintage
French style with relaxed Southern comfort. Her airy
master suite, with its serene aqua walls and billowing
curtains, is a retreat where linen sheets are perfumed
with powder, and a feather bed is fluffed to perfection.
"Many times, the things that I love do not hold any
extraordinary value," she says. "It is just the perfect
patina or a feeling of happiness when I see it."

"Now I really feel the landscape, I can be bold and include every tone of blue and pink: it's enchanting, it's delicious."

—Claude Monet

This dining-room table—a roomy English reproduction paired with Chippendale-style chairs—showcases a trio of blue-and-white vases brimming with sprays of fresh pink tulips. The lavish Heriz rug beneath reiterates the homeowner's preferred palette of pink and blue.

Set against a backdrop of lush greens, a veranda set for an alfresco tea party promises a festive afternoon amid a tableau of lovely hues. A gleaming silver service, pristine white linens, and a classic transferware pattern add an air of formality to the occasion, but the addition of vivid pink blooms brings a welcome touch of playfulness to the gathering. Whether paired with other colors or enjoyed in its purity, no matter the season or celebration, beauty is assured in the enduring palette of blue and white.

CREDITS & RESOURCES

Living with Blue & White

Editor-in-Chief: Phyllis Hoffman DePiano

Editor: Jordan Marxer Millner

Managing Editor: Melissa Lester

Associate Editor: Karen Callaway

Assistant Editor: Leslie Bennett Smith

Art Director: Tracy Wood-Franklin

Stylist: Melissa Sturdivant Smith

Editorial Assistant: Kassidy Abernathy

Creative Director/Photography: Mac Jamieson

Senior Copy Editor: Rhonda Lee Lother

Senior Digital Imaging Specialist: Delisa McDaniel

CONTRIBUTING WRITERS

JEANNE DELATHOUDER: pages 13–14

CONTRIBUTING PHOTOGRAPHERS

KIMBERLY FINKEL DAVIS: pages 177, 180–183, 185, 196–198, 200–201 and 246

BRITTANY WILLIAMS FLOWERS: pages 44, 70 and 73–75

CORRINE JAMET: pages 102–107

JOHN O'HAGAN: pages 2, 43, 68–69, 88, 90, 138, 160–161, 204–205, 238–239, 245 and back cover

TOSHI OTSUKI: pages 33, 39, 41, 54–55, 60–61, 64–67, 80–81, 89, 95–96, 127, 148–153, 166–167, 177, 220, 223 and 226

STEVEN RANDAZZO: pages 89, 91–92, 94, 126, 222 and 226

KATE SEARS: pages 108, 120–121, 139, 162–163 and 173

MARCY BLACK SIMPSON: Cover and pages 4–5, 8, 12–20, 22–23, 26–27, 32, 34–35, 38, 40, 46, 56–57, 71, 78, 82–87, 96–101, 128–129, 133, 137, 140–141, 155–159, 164–165, 168–169, 172, 194–195, 202–203, 208, 210–211, 213, 215–216, 218–220, 226, 228–231, 232, 237, 240–241 and 246

MICHAEL SKOTT: page 50

STEPHANIE WELBOURNE STEELE: pages 22–23, 28–29, 31, 37, 43, 52, 58–59, 130–131, 146, 177, 184, 190–193, 213, 220–221, 225, 234, 236, 244, 251 and 256

CONTRIBUTING STYLISTS

MISSIE NEVILLE CRAWFORD: pages 62–63, 78, 82–87 and 237

MARIE-PAULE FAURE: pages 102–107

BRITTANY WILLIAMS FLOWERS: Pages 44, 70, 73–75, 108, 120–121 and 139

TESSA FOLEY: pages 2, 43, 68–69, 88, 90, 138, 160–161 and 245

ANNA GILMORE: Cover and page 32

MARY LEIGH GWALTNEY: pages 4–8, 10, 12–20, 22–23, 29, 34–35, 38, 40, 46, 48–49, 56–57, 64–65, 133, 137, 194–195, 208, 210–211, 213, 215–216, 218–220, 230–232, 240, 246–247, 251 and 256

LINDSAY KEITH KESSLER: page 139

YUKIE MCLEAN: pages 71, 112–119, 136, 165, 168–169, 180, 182–183, 185, 196–198, 200–203 and 228–229

KATHLEEN COOK VARNER: pages 98–101, 172, 234, 237 and 241

JAN WARE: pages 130–131

WHERE TO SHOP & BUY

Below is a list of products and companies featured in this book.

Pages 12–20: L. Craig Roberts, AIA, 146 Westfield Ave., Mobile, AL, 251-343-8165, lcraigroberts.com.

Pages 22–23 and 29: For more information about Jane Marsden Antiques & Interiors, visit marsdenantiques.com.

Page 24: L. V. Harkness & Company: John Morris Custom Hand Painted Pillow, 866-225-7474, lvharkness.com.

Page 25: Caitlin Wilson Design: Highland Floral Wallpaper; 866-409-7216, caitlinwilson.com. Kelby's Original Art: *Hydrangea Study III*, *Hydrangea Study IV*; 478-320-3182, kelbyoriginals.com. Tessitura Pardi: Raso Unito Rustica Tablecloth in Navy, Botticelli Navy Blue Rustica Linen Tablecloth; from Beautiful Linens, 844-546-3671, beautifullinens.com. Rizzoli: *Authentic Design: Lauren Rottet and Rottet Studio* by Lauren Rottet, *An Eye for Beauty: Rooms That Speak to the Senses* by Beth Webb; 800-522-6657, rizzolibookstore.com. CICO Books: *William Yeoward: Blue & White and Other Stories* by William Yeoward; 646-791-5410, rylandpeters.com.

Pages 28, 31 and 244: Special thanks to interior designer, florist, and stylist Ryan Dunagan at Ryan Studio Interiors, ryan@ryanstudio.net.

Pages 30 and 248–249: For more information on Carolyn Westbrook, visit facebook.com/Carolyn-Westbrook-Home-115385071836527/ or email cwestbrookhome@airmail.net.

Page 32: Farrow & Ball: St. Antoine BP 946; 888-511-1121, farrow-ball.com.

Page 37: Designers Guild: Roseto Wallpaper in Indigo, Damasco Wallpaper in Gold, Floreale Wallpaper in Celadon; designersguild.com.

Page 38: Pat Kerr Designs: Baby & Children's Couture, Cocktail & Ballgown Couture, and Bridal Couture. Pat Kerr, Inc., 901-525-5223, pattkerr.com, patkerrinc@patkerr.com.

Page 40: Brunschwig & Fils: Festival of Lanterns in Powder Blue, Verrieres fabric in Shades of Blue; Lee Jofa: Cliffoney Blue/White; kravet.com. Jane Churchill: Bruton Damask fabric in Blue/ Beige, Malory Wallpaper in Blue; from Cowtan & Tout, designs.cowtan.com.

Pages 2, 43, 68–69, 88, 90, 138, 160–161 and 245: For more information about Tessa Foley, visit her website, nineandsixteen.com.

Page 46: Johnson Brothers: Devon Cottage Dinner Plate, Devon Cottage Salad Plate; from Belk, 866-235-5443, belk.com. Christofle: Aria 6-piece place setting; christofle.com. Waterford: Araglin Tea Glass; from

Bromberg's, 205-871-3276, brombergs.com.

Page 48: Herend: Chinese Bouquet Teacup, Chinese Bouquet Saucer; 800-643-7363, herendusa.com. Mottahedeh: Blue Lace Pitcher, Blue Lace Service Plate, Blue Lace Cup and Saucer; mottahedeh.com. Empire Silver: Sterling Salt Cellars; Reed & Barton: Francis I Spoons; Waterford: Lismore Water Goblet; from Bromberg's, 205-871-3276, brombergs.com.

Pages 48–49: Royal Crown Derby: Aves Blue Salad Plate, Aves Blue Tea Cup, Aves Blue Saucer, Aves Blue Teapot, Aves Blue Sugar Bowl, Aves Blue Creamer; royalcrownderby.co.uk.

Page 49: Varga: Athens Sky Blue Champagne flute; from Gracious Style, graciousstyle.com.

Page 52: Port 68: Summer Palace Basin, Summer Palace Lamp 36"H; Williamsburg for Port 68: Braganza Blue Large Jar; 866-960-7930, port68.com. Hester & Cook: Die-Cut China Blue Vase Card, China Blue Acanthus Placemats, Painted Check Paper Table Runner, China Blue Acanthus Wine Bag, China Blue Acanthus Cub Bag, China Blue Paper Table Runner; 615-736-2892, hesterandcook.com.

Pages 52 and 58–59: Royal Crown Derby: Blue Mikado Luncheon Plate, Blue Mikado Rim Soup Bowl, Blue Mikado Mini Creamer, Blue Mikado Flat Cup & Saucer Set, Blue Mikado Teapot & Lid; from Replacements, Ltd., 800-737-5223, replacements.com. Royal Crown Derby: Grenville Dinner Plate, Grenville Rim Soup Bowl, Royal Crown Derby: Grenville Tea Cup, Grenville Tea Saucer; from DeVine Corporation, 732-751-0500, devinecorp.net.

Page 56: J. Seignolles: Arborescence Tea Cup & Saucer, Arborescence Dinner Plate; Mottahedeh: Blue Lace Service Plate; Bernardaud: Grace Tea Cup, Grace Saucer, Grace Salad Plate, Grace Dinner Plate; Wedgwood: Anthemion Blue Champagne Flute, Anthemion Blue 5-piece place setting; Moser: Maharani White Wine Glass; from Bromberg's, 205-871-3276, brombergs.com.

Pages 56 57: Apilco: Tradition Blue-Banded Porcelain Dinner Plate; from Williams-Sonoma, 877-812-6235, williams-sonoma.com. Christofle Aria 6-Piece Place Setting; christofle.com. Market Street Candles; 310-977-9795, marketstreetcandles.com.

Pages 62–63: Fostoria: Navarre Blue Water Goblet; from Replacements, Ltd., 800-737-5223, replacements.com. Sasha Nicholas: Weave Monogrammed Soup Bowl, Weave Monogrammed Salad Plate, Weave Monogrammed Dinner Plate, Weave Monogrammed Charger/Dinner Plate, Gold-Rimmed Charger with Monogram; 888-877-5230, sashanicholas.com.

Page 63: Williams-Sonoma Vintage Floral Jacquard Place Mats, 877-812-6235, williams-sonoma.com. Vietri: Aladdin Blue Antique 5-Piece Place Setting in Blue; 919-245-4180, vietri.com. Beauville: Rialto Blue Napkins; 847-518-1232, yvonne-estelles.com.

Page 75: Anna Bove Embroidery, annaboveembroidery.com.

Pages 98–101: Interior design by Phoebe Howard, 404-816-3830, phoebehoward.net.

Pages 102–107: Adriana Anzola, etsy.com/shop/myshabbywhites, @shabby_whites on Instagram.

Page 133: Pom Pom at Home, 818-847-0150, pompomathome.com.

Page 137: Skyros Designs, 901-762-0377, skyrosdesigns.com.

Page 146: Ralph Lauren Home: Darian Tea Tray, Darian Tea Set; 888-475-7674, ralphlauren.com. Vista Alegre: Transatlântica Tea Cup & Saucer, Transatlântica Tall Pot with Lid, Transatlântica Low Pot with Lid; 888-506-0526, vistaalegre.com.

Page 147: Eastern Accents: Badu Beanstalk lumbar pillow with insert, Badu Beanstalk decorative pillow with cord; 800-282-1671, easternaccents.com.

Pages 155–159: Danny O'Bryant, Dan's Picture Framing and Design, luv2sellart@gmail.com. Hamilton Collection: America's Greatest Sailing Ships Eagle Plate, America's Greatest Sailing Ships Bonhomme Richard Plate; from Replacements, Ltd., 800-737-5223, replacements.com.

Page 165: Artwork by Itsuko McKinney, itsukomckinney.myportfolio.com.

Pages 170–171, 174–175: Gien: Oiseau Bleu 5 Piece Setting, Pivoines Bleues Creamer, Pivoines Bleues Sugar Bowl, Pivoines Bleues Teapot; 800-834-3797, fxdougherty.com. Indigo Home Shop, LLC: Initial Ginger Jar Napkin Ring; indigohomeshop.com. Hermès: Bleus d'Ailleurs Dessert Plate; 800-441-4488, hermes.com.

Page 171: Danny's Fine Porcelain: Blue and White Hexagonal Lidded Jar, Blue and White Rectangular Lidded Box, Blue and White Porcelain Jar with Antique Finish; 214-638-8382, dannysporcelain.com.

Page 194: Williams Sonoma: Alton 5-Piece Flatware, 877-812-6235, williams-sonoma.com.

Pages 202–203: Wedgwood: Blue Jasper Small Vase, 877-720-3486, wedgwoodusa.com.

Pages 204–205 and 238–239: For more information about interior designer Marsha Mason and her collections, visit her Instagram, @marshamason2, marsha@wildwooddesign.net.

Page 210: Herend: Chinese Bouquet Blue Tea Cup, Chinese Blue Tea Saucer; 800-643-7363, herendusa.com.

Page 212: Royal Copenhagen: Blue Fluted Plain Flat Cup and Saucer Set, Mega Blue Fluted Blue Fluted Tea Pot and Lid, Blue Fluted Half Lace Border Jug; from Replacements, Ltd., 800-737-5223, replacements.com.

Pages 213 and 220: Haute Papier, 866-740-4222, hautepapier.com.

Page 216: Spode: Blue Italian Tea Cup & Saucer, 888-778-1471, spode.com.

Page 220: Herend: Chinese Bouquet Blue Oval Box, 800-643-7363, herendusa.com.

Page 221: Yves Delorme; 800-322-3911, usa.yvesdelorme.com. D. Porthault, 212-688-1660, dporthaultparis.com.

Page 236: Peacock Alley, 800-496-2880, peacockalley.com. Pottery Barn, 888-779-5176, potterybarn.com. Serena & Lily, 866-597-2742, serenaandlily.com.

Page 252–253: Johnson Brothers: Willow Blue Dinner Plate, Willow Blue Salad Plate, Willow Blue Flat Cup & Saucer Set; Gorham: Versailles New French Hollow Knife, Versailles Fork, Versailles Teaspoon; from Replacements, Ltd., 800-737-5223, replacements.com.